DETROIT PUBLIC LIBRARY
3 5674 0094687

D1090639

SCIENCE STORY LIBRARY

Young children can grasp scientific concepts and are interested in the world they live in. The Science Story Library is designed to answer this interest. The books present important scientific events and tell the lives of great men of science. They offer concepts meaningful to children through good—and scientifically accurate—storytelling. The series is illustrated by leading American artists.

BENJAMIN FRANKLIN, SCIENTIST-DIPLOMAT
By Charles Michael Daugherty / Illustrated by John Falter

ROBERT GODDARD, TRAIL BLAZER TO THE STARS
By Charles Michael Daugherty / Illustrated by James Daugherty

ARCHIMEDES, MATHEMATICIAN AND INVENTOR
By Martin Gardner / Illustrated by Leonard Everett Fisher

GALILEO GALILEI, SPACE PIONEER
By Arthur S. Gregor / Illustrated by James W. Williamson

SIGMUND FREUD, DOCTOR OF SECRETS AND DREAMS
By John Mann / Illustrated by Clare Romano Ross and John Ross

SIR ARTHUR EVANS, DISCOVERER OF KNOSSOS
By George Selden / Illustrated by Lee Ames

HEINRICH SCHLIEMANN, DISCOVERER OF BURIED TREASURE
By George Selden / Illustrated by Lorence F. Bjorklund

ALEXANDER THE GREAT, SCIENTIST-KING
By Robert C. Suggs / Illustrated by Leonard Everett Fisher

J. Falter

Benjamin Franklin

SCIENTIST-DIPLOMAT

BY

CHARLES MICHAEL DAUGHERTY

ILLUSTRATED BY JOHN FALTER

THE MACMILLAN COMPANY, NEW YORK

COLLIER-MACMILLAN LIMITED, LONDON

Library of Congress catalog card number: 64-22798

First printing

The Macmillan Company, New York
Collier-Macmillan Canada, Ltd., Toronto, Ontario

Designed by Hilda Scott

Printed in the United States of America

Benjamin Franklin

SCIENTIST-DIPLOMAT

JF

In 1740, when Benjamin Franklin was a young man, and already famous, the American colonies still belonged to England. He was a successful printer and writer, a publisher of newspapers and books, and the Postmaster of Philadelphia. But above all, he was famous as an inventor and scientist, or natural philosopher, as scientists were then called. This is the story of Benjamin Franklin, scientist and inventor.

Franklin was born in 1706 in Boston, capital of the colony of Massachusetts, and at that time the biggest, busiest, and most important town in America.

His father, Josiah Franklin, was a maker of soap and candles. There was no such thing as electric light in those days. Nobody knew much about the mysterious force called electricity, nor dreamed of the uses to which it would be put one day. Every house was lighted by oil lamps and candles; so were all the public buildings. As a result, when people in Boston needed new candles, they hurried to the house in Milk Street where Josiah Franklin had his shop. He also had his living quarters there—*and* his wife and their fifteen children. From breakfast to bedtime, the crowded rooms were full of running, jumping, wriggling, giggling brothers and sisters, and often their cousins and playmates by the dozens.

A blue globe hung over the door instead of a printed sign. It was easy to see and helped customers find the shop. Because so few people could read in the early 18th century, all shops displayed the symbols of their trades.

There were ten boys in the Franklin family, and five girls. Ben was the youngest of the boys. He was also the brightest. He learned to read by himself almost as soon as he was old enough to talk. There were many other things he liked to do as well as read. He was strong as a young bear, a fine swimmer, and good at all kinds of games.

When he was eight years old, Ben went to school. And since he was so bright and full of curiosity, he was soon at the head of his class.

His mother and father were proud of him. "I do believe our Ben is going to be a scholar and a gentleman," Josiah told friends and relatives. "Perhaps he'll even become a minister of the church."

But to become a minister, Ben would have to go to school for many years. Josiah Franklin, with a big family to take care of, finally decided that he could not afford the expense of so much schooling. After the boy had been in school only a year, his father decided to keep him home and teach him to make candles. At least he would have a trade.

Instead of studying Latin and arithmetic, Ben cut

wicks and melted wax. But though he no longer went to school he was so curious about the world, and so eager to understand it, that he kept on reading and learning by himself.

Even at play he was alert and quick to learn. Often his curiosity led him to try new and better ways of doing things. For instance, he loved swimming, and one summer day he thought of a new way to make himself move through the water.

He made two oval-shaped paddles out of wood. That was one improvement! If he held one firmly in each hand, he could swim much faster than any of his playmates. He then made another pair of wooden fin-shaped paddles and strapped these to his feet, just as skin divers now wear rubber fins for swimming under water. These wooden paddles were Ben Franklin's first invention.

Another of Ben's recreations was kite-flying. How pleasant it would be, he thought, to go swimming and fly a kite at the same time. So he took off his clothes and, holding on to the string of his kite, plunged into the water. As he floated on his back the kite towed him gently across the pond.

"There," a friend of his said, "that's Ben. He's always thinking of new ways to do things."

"Yes," another playmate answered, "and then we wonder why *we* didn't think of them."

Although Ben helped his father in the shop, he decided he didn't want to make candles all his life. He thought it would be much more fun to become a sailor, and go to sea, as one of his older brothers had done.

But Ben's father believed that a boy who loved books and learning was meant for something better than the rough life of a sailor. One day he took Ben for a walk around the town, so that the boy could see all the workmen at their jobs, and decide for himself what he would like to do when he grew up.

They watched the shopkeepers in their shops, the blacksmiths shoeing horses, the printers at the press, the carpenters and the bricklayers building houses, the butchers selling meat, and the bakers baking bread. When they had seen them all, Mr. Franklin turned to Ben and asked, "Which do you like most?"

Ben thought hard. "I believe I like one as much as the other," he said.

"But what trade do you think you'd most like to follow?"

"I can't say. I like them all, Father," insisted Ben.

So his father had to make the boy's mind up for him. He decided, because Ben liked books, that he should

be a printer. James, an older brother, had a printing business in Boston. "You can go to work for James," Mr. Franklin said, "and learn the printer's trade."

In his printing shop, James Franklin published a newspaper, *The New England Courant.* At first, Ben helped by sweeping the floor, running errands, and

delivering papers. Before long, he was able to set type. As time went by, and he learned the publishing business, he became eager to try his hand at writing for the newspaper.

Ben was afraid that James would not publish anything written by a fifteen-year-old, so he thought of a plan. He would fool James into believing that what he himself wrote was really written by someone else. At night, after work, Ben wrote a letter to the newspaper, like the ones printed in today's papers. When it was finished, he signed it Silence Dogwood, a name that he made up. What's more, "Silence" was a woman's name—so he really had a double disguise.

James found the letter under the door when he opened the shop in the morning. "Sir," it began, "it may not be improper in the first place to inform your Readers, that I intend . . . to present them, by the help of this Paper, with a short Epistle, which I presume will add somewhat to their Entertainment."

The rest of the letter, and other Silence Dogwood letters that soon followed, talked about schooling, writing, poetry, and anything else Ben found interesting. James Franklin thought them wise and witty. Many of his paper's readers liked them too. Nobody guessed that the writer was the publisher's younger brother.

Ben was a hard worker, but he and his brother were not always as friendly as they might have been. At times James was a harsh master.

Once, when James got in trouble with some of the important people in Boston because something that he had printed disagreed with their ideas, he was sent to jail for a month. Ben ran the newspaper. And, although he made a good job of it, when James returned there was trouble again between the brothers, and they quarreled harder than ever. Their father tried to straighten things out, but even he couldn't help, and the two kept right on arguing. There were even times when James beat his younger brother. Benjamin could stand it no longer. One day, without saying good-bye to anyone, he ran away from Boston. He made his way to Philadelphia, in the colony of Pennsylvania. He had heard so much about it that he thought he might be happy there.

1 Mi. to P.
JF

When Ben went to Philadelphia, he was seventeen years old. He soon found a job as a printer's helper. The City of Brotherly Love, as Philadelphia is often called, was a busy, growing town, and Benjamin Franklin, turning from a sturdy boy into an ambitious young man, grew with it. He made important friends, read continually, and continued to educate himself. And he traveled across the ocean to England. For a year and a half he lived in London, where he improved his skill as a printer and where he learned something more of the world he loved so much.

However, Philadelphia was the city in which he wanted to make his home, and it was to Philadelphia that he returned. Now twenty years old, he had a thorough knowledge of the printing business, and a clear idea of the course he wanted to follow. The years

ahead were crowded ones. At twenty-four, he married Deborah Read, a Philadelphia girl whom he had known since he first arrived in that city. They moved into a new house and, using part of it as a shop, Benjamin was able to work at his printing while Deborah kept a store where she sold paper, ink, and books.

Often neighbors saw a light burning late at night in Ben's workroom. "That young man is full of promise," one said to another. "He's a hard worker. I hear he's even taught himself a lot of that foreign talk."

Another acquaintance agreed. "Latin, I've heard. And French, Spanish, and Italian, too."

"I guess if a man really wants to learn, he will," said a third.

The year before his marriage, Ben Franklin had started a newspaper, called *The Pennsylvania Gazette*. Most of what was said in it he wrote himself, but perhaps it was so important because it was the springboard for his *Poor Richard's Almanac*. This was a series of paperbound books published at the beginning of each year. In a way, they were more interesting than his job as Philadelphia's Postmaster, a post to which he had recently been appointed. In the *Almanac*, Ben could say what he thought—not only about the weather—but about everything else that struck his fancy. He

predicted the weather for the next twelve months, gave information on the daily tides, and told people when the moon would change. Along with this valuable knowledge, Ben also included the jokes, poems, and wise sayings readers had liked so much when he worked on *The Courant*.

"Poor Richard's" popularity grew rapidly. Farmers,

boatmen, travelers, and many other people all over the country bought the *Almanac* and found it helpful—and exciting. They laughed at the jokes and made the wise sayings part of the language we use today. Families, gathered around the fire on winter evenings, read aloud from the pages, where they might find:

Early to bed, and early to rise,
Makes a man healthy, wealthy, and wise.

or

Would you live with ease, do what you ought,
not what you please.

or

The noblest question in the world is,
"What good may I do in it?"

The first to practice what "Poor Richard" preached was Ben himself. No matter how hard he worked he found time to study and, above all, he tried to follow his own advice. And just as his curiosity had led him to use wooden paddles for swimming when he was a boy, he wanted to find new and better ways of doing and making things. He must help people be more comfortable as they went about their jobs.

He wondered, for instance, if the *colors* of clothes worn by men and women might have something to do

Poor Richard, 1731.
AN
Almanack
1731

with how warm they might be in winter or how cool they might keep in summer. In order to find out, he tried some tests, or experiments.

As usual, Ben felt he had to find out for himself.

One sunny winter day, Ben took bits of colored cloth —black, blue, purple, green, red, yellow, white—and laid them side by side on top of the snow. After several

hours he found that some had sunk into the snow while others still were lying on top. The black cloth had sunk the deepest. The sun had made it so warm that the snow on which it lay had melted beneath it. The blue cloth had also displaced snow, but not as much as the black. And the lighter the color of the cloth, the smaller the impression it had made on the snow. As a result,

the bit of white cloth was still on top, just as he had left it.

By this experiment, Franklin proved that dark materials absorb, or soak up, the sun's rays and become warmer than do white, or light-colored, materials. What he had learned he put to good use. He pointed out that for comfort's sake the color of people's clothes should be suited to the weather: to keep warm in winter, black was the best choice; to keep cool in summer, white, or pastel shades, were more comfortable.

To make living more convenient, Franklin also thought of a new kind of stove. Open fireplaces were then used to heat houses, and it took a lot of wood to keep them going. But Franklin's stove was made of iron. It needed less wood than most fireplaces, and yet it produced more heat because the flames were contained in a snug metal firebox.

Ben called his stove the Pennsylvania fireplace and

used it in his own house. Soon many other families were using it too. It became known as the Franklin stove. Even today, stoves of this type are sometimes used instead of fireplaces in country houses that have no furnaces, or homes that need extra protection from the cold.

In Philadelphia, Benjamin Franklin was becoming a person of importance. He was a well-educated man (even though he had taught himself), and also one of the wealthiest. He no longer had to run his printing press, but could hire others to do the work for him.

He was free to spend his time as he pleased, and nothing pleased him more than studying, learning, and continuing his never-ending experiments.

There was hardly a subject that did *not* interest him. He studied the weather to learn the cause behind storms. He watched colonies of ants, and believed that they might have some way of talking to each other. He bought a farm and was one of the first landowners in America to try raising crops scientifically. Everything he saw or heard invited him to take notice and think, "How interesting! I wish I knew more about that." And whenever it was possible, he took the time and trouble to find out more, even though it meant years of work and study, as it did when he made up his mind to learn more about "electrical fluid," or electricity, as it was known in the eighteenth century.

The mystery behind electricity fascinated Ben Franklin, along with other philosophers and scientists of the time. One day in 1746, while he was on a visit to his old home in Boston, he met a doctor named Spence, from Scotland. Dr. Spence talked a great deal about electricity, and he had brought with him a machine that could give out electric sparks.

It was the first time Franklin had seen such a machine. He was so pleased with it that he bought it from

Dr. Spence and took it back with him to Philadelphia.

Now the question "What *is* electricity?" became the most important problem in his busy life. Many other wise men in various countries had puzzled for a long time over the same question. They had found that if a ball made of glass or sulphur were rubbed with the hand, the ball then had a power that attracted light-weight items like feathers, bits of paper, or straw. This force could not be seen but natural philosophers who studied it had learned that it flowed from one object to another, and as it did, it sometimes made sparks that *could* be seen. In fact, they looked like tiny, jagged streaks of lightning.

The machine that Franklin brought home from Boston was a glass tube with a crank at one end. When he put a hand against the tube, and turned the crank with his other hand, he could cause sparks to appear. If he then touched anyone standing nearby, he or she was likely to feel a small shock as the electricity flowed from one body to another.

Day after day, as pleased as a boy with a new toy, Ben Franklin turned and rubbed the glass tube. He wanted to find out just how the electricity it made acted on glass and metal, on cloth and wood, on things that were cold or hot, wet or dry.

Many friends came to his house to watch these tests. He had let it be known, just before Christmas, that he was going to kill a turkey by electric shock! The force of the electricity, he explained, might make the meat tender. A great many people gathered to see the experiment. They crowded around the scientist as he attached the wires to the bird, talking and asking so many questions that Franklin was unable to pay close attention to what he was doing. All of a sudden there was a loud crack, like a pistol shot, and a flash of fire.

"Heaven help us!" cried a frightened watcher.

"Where's a doctor?" shouted another.

The shock had struck Mr. Franklin instead of the bird. He fell to the floor and lay as though dead. But he soon opened his eyes and sat up. He was pale and shaking, but he was able to laugh about what had happened. "I had meant to kill a turkey," he said, "and I almost killed a goose." It was his way of admitting that he had been careless and foolish.

Ben Franklin's attempt to kill a turkey electrically had gone wrong and nearly killed him, but he had learned a great deal from his many experiments, and he knew more about electricity than any other scientist of his time. When, during a thunderstorm, he watched the clouds flash streaks of fire, he saw a likeness between the lightning and electric sparks. He was sure that he had found the answer to the question "What is lightning?"

"Lightning," he said, "is nothing more than electricity."

Others had already said the same thing but nobody had yet been able to offer any proof. Franklin set out to prove he was right.

JF

First he wrote a list of all the things that made lightning and electricity seem the same:

1. Both gave light.
2. Their light was the same color.
3. Both traveled in an irregular pattern.
4. Both made a swift flash.
5. Both were attracted to metals and flowed freely through metal.
6. Both could melt metal.
7. Both could cause other materials to burn.
8. Both sometimes made loud crackling sounds, something like small explosions.
9. Both could flow through water and ice.
10. Both could break or twist the objects they passed through.
11. Both could kill living things.
12. Both smelled the same.

He also thought of another experiment and wrote a paper describing it. These were his instructions: On top of a high tower or steeple, build a platform large enough to hold a man. Let a long iron rod, pointed at the top, rise into the air from the platform. Should a storm come up, the electrical "fire" will flow from the clouds into the rod, due to the fact that metal attracts electricity. A man, standing on the platform during the storm, would be able to see sparks and hear their crackling sound, but to make sure he isn't hurt himself, he should see to it that a wire runs from the rod to the ground in order to carry off the electricity.

These instructions were read by men of learning in France and England as well as in America. A French scientist named Thomas-François Dalibard was the first to put them to practice. In a garden near Paris, he set a long iron rod upright on a wooden plank. As soon as a storm arose the rod began to sparkle and crackle with electricity, just as Benjamin Franklin had written that it would.

The news of Dalibard's success was exciting to everybody who cared about science and progress. His name was on many lips all over Europe, where his experiment was repeated by other scientists. But it was Benjamin Franklin who got the credit for a big forward step in understanding electrical current. Even the King of France praised him, and ordered that a letter of thanks be sent to "Mr. Franklin in Philadelphia."

News crossed the ocean in sailing ships and took a long time to reach the other side. Not dreaming that a letter from a king was on the way to him, or that his experiment had already been done by other scientists,

JF

“Mr. Franklin in Philadelphia” was getting ready to try gathering electricity from the sky.

He still thought that he needed a tower or steeple in order to get close to the clouds. But there was no spire in Philadelphia high enough to suit him. As he tried to think of some way of reaching into the clouds he remembered how, when he was a boy in Boston, he had floated on his back in the water and been towed across the pond by a kite.

A kite with a long string could reach higher than any steeple ever built. He would attach a bit of metal, such as an iron door key, to the lower end of the string, so that if the kite drew electricity from the clouds it would be attracted by the metal and flow down through the string.

It had been a long time since Ben last flew a kite. Now that he was a grown man what would the neighbors think to see him playing a children’s game? In order to avoid their questions, and to have plenty of room for his experiment, he walked out of town into the fields with only his son, William, for company.

JF

There were dark clouds overhead and they could hear thunder growling as they left the town's boundaries. The two kite fliers gave their kite more string as it rode high on the wind. At the lower end of the string, where it could be reached and tested for a spark, hung an iron key.

The kite bobbed and tugged at the end of its string, but no electricity was attracted to it. At last, when the Franklins were almost ready to give up and go home, they saw that the fibers of the string were moving and standing on end, as though they were alive. Mr. Franklin reached toward the key—something only a trained scientist should ever do—and as his hand came close to it he saw and felt a spark jump, just like the sparks that crackled from the glass tube of his electrical machine when he rubbed it.

Now the rain really began to fall. As the kite string got wet, more and bigger sparks came from the key. Fortunately, the electricity that flowed that day from the clouds to Ben Franklin's kite, and down the string to the key near his hand, was not strong enough to hurt him. After the storm he and William, drenched but happy, returned to town. As they walked through the wet grass the father's mind was busy thinking how he might put to use what he had learned—for he had learned something. The kite and the string had had to become thoroughly wet before the lightning was strongly attracted to it. And, as usual, he thought of something that might help *many* people.

In the next issue of *Poor Richard's Almanac* he wrote of his newest invention and gave directions so that everybody who cared to could make use of it. He instructed his subscribers to attach a long iron rod to the side of a house, so that the lower end of the rod was in the ground. The other end should rise six or eight inches above the roof. Then, if lightning struck, it would be attracted by the pointed rod and would run into the ground without doing damage to the house or the people who lived there.

As soon as Franklin's readers realized that this simple device would protect their homes, they began to do as their *Almanacs* told them. Nobody knows how many houses and barns and human lives have been

saved by Franklin's lightning rod, but after two hundred years, the number continues to grow every time there is a thunderstorm.

In many countries, wherever men and women gathered in each other's houses to plan for a better world, they often talked about the printer from Philadelphia who had become a scientist and later a representative of his new country to the old world of Europe. He gave many years to serving in the battle for freedom from English rule, and when the Revolution-

ary War was over, he took a leading part in forming the new government of the United States.

Politics often kept him so busy that he had to put aside the scientific work he enjoyed more than anything else. But whenever he had a few hours or days to spare, he used the time to explore the mysteries of

nature, to experiment, and to exchange ideas with other scientists.

Aboard ship, on the voyages he made to England and France, he spent his time studying the ocean and observing its currents. Franklin was the first scientist to make a study of the Gulf Stream. This current flows like a great river across the Atlantic Ocean from the Gulf of Mexico to the shores of northern Europe. As a result of his findings, he was able to advise ships' captains that they could make faster crossings to ports in America by staying away from the Gulf Stream.

In appreciation for all the work he had done for his fellow men, Benjamin Franklin was awarded many of the world's highest honors. Yale and Harvard gave him degrees, and academies of learning and science in England, France, and Spain made him a member. All over the world, people not only admired and praised him, but loved him as though he were a kind and helpful friend.

And because his achievements were so many, and so great, Benjamin Franklin's death on April 17, 1790, seemed to rob the world of a number of great men. And the people who mourned him felt a heavy loss indeed; "Poor Richard" had meant so much in their everyday lives.

JF

This marble statue of Benjamin Franklin, four times life size, was sculpted by James Earle Fraser. It stands in the Memorial Hall of the Franklin Institute in Philadelphia, which is dedicated to research and public education in the physical sciences. It is fitting that this Institute should be named for the man who played such an important role in American science.

ABOUT THE AUTHOR: Charles Michael Daugherty began his career as a professional artist and book illustrator but is now devoting all of his time to writing, primarily books on scientific subjects. He studied at the Yale University School of Fine Arts and the Art Students League of New York. He has traveled widely, served as Staff Photographer for the Inca Highway archaeological expedition in 1953, and in preparation of his book *City Under the Ice, The Story of Camp Century,* spent over a month in Greenland studying this project. Among his other recent books are *Searchers of the Sea, The Great Archaeologists,* and another Macmillan Science Story Library book, *Robert Goddard, Trail Blazer to the Stars.* Mr. Daugherty and his wife live in New York City.

ABOUT THE ILLUSTRATOR: John Philip Falter was born in Plattsmouth, Nebraska. Upon completion of his studies at the Kansas City Art Institute, he was awarded the New York Art Students League scholarship. In addition to his classes at the Art Students League, he took night classes at Grand Central Art School. He began his professional career illustrating covers for magazines such as *Western Stories* and *Detective Magazine.* Since then, his illustrations have appeared in many magazines, including the *Saturday Evening Post* where he has been a cover artist since 1944. His book work includes five other Macmillan books, *The Adventures of Tom Sawyer, The Adventures of Huckleberry Finn, The Scarlet Pimpernel, Me 'n' Steve,* and *Treasure Island,* for which he received an award from the Society of Illustrators.